DAISY

The True Story of an Amazing 3-Legged Chinchilla

By Marney Studaker-Cordner
and
Kimberly Abraham

www.therapiesinapod.com

ISBN: 0615891403
ISBN 13: 9780615891408
Library of Congress Control Number: 2013917808
Studaker Enterprises Inc, Attica, MI

Dedication:

This book is dedicated to individuals and families everywhere, who meet the challenges of living with physical differences every day with courage and love.For Faith, whose love for Daisy transcended trauma and helped her heal.

The authors wish to thank:

The fabulous staff at Veterinary Care Specialists in Milford, Michigan. We are so grateful for the care and love you gave Daisy. You're the best!

Elizabeth Coyle, who said, "Why don't you write a book?" Thanks Aunt Lil, not only for the idea but for your love and support every day of my life.

Martha Studaker, for racing to the animal emergency room with me at midnight and Rodney Studaker for Rosie's poem.

Special thanks to Ryan Haack, www.livingonehanded.com, for your kind words about Daisy's story. You're an inspiration!

Brenda and Dani Vossen of MiChubby Chins in Port Huron, Michigan for looking through your picture collection and for bringing Daisy and Rosie into our lives.

Red at Artistic Images in Imlay City, Michigan for the wonderful photos of our chinchillas.

Courtney Cordner, for the fantastic cover and interior design.

My name is Rosie and I'm a chinchilla. When I was a baby, I was adopted by a twelve-year-old girl named Faith.

Faith loves me very much and would play with me every day. But sometimes I got lonely, especially at night.

So one day, Faith brought home another chinchilla, named Daisy, to live with me. Daisy was younger and smaller than me, so I felt like it was my job to protect her and keep her safe.

We became best friends. We slept right next to each other, ran and played every day.

Because Daisy and I have fur coats, we can get too hot, very fast. One summer it was too warm in Faith's room, so Daisy and I moved to a chinchilla house downstairs, where we could stay cool.

We had only been there a week when all of a sudden... Daisy caught her leg in the cage and fell! Faith and her mom rushed Daisy to the animal hospital and I had to stay home. I was so worried about Daisy and afraid of what would happen to her.

8

She was gone for three days, and when she came back, she looked different. She only had three legs! Daisy told me about how she'd gone to the hospital and the doctor operated to save her life. But in order to save her, they had to remove her broken back leg. They called it an amputation.

9

10

I love Daisy so much and was happy she was alive! But to tell you the truth, she looked kind of funny...

She had a cone around her neck to keep her from chewing on her stitches. It looked like a big UFO around her head!

12

When Daisy ate, sometimes the food fell down inside her cone. That made her grumpy! She couldn't hold her raisins so Faith had to feed them to her.

14

And sometimes when she was sitting down, she would lean to one side – or even tip right over – because there was no leg there to hold her up.

16

She would look around to see if anyone saw her fall and I always pretended to be looking up at the ceiling or out the window, like I hadn't noticed. I didn't want her to be embarrassed, but she would just laugh and pick herself back up...

18

Daisy had to take medicine and be very careful for a little while. She wasn't allowed to run or jump. Sometimes that made her frustrated and sad. She would "chitter" at Faith to let her play.

Faith would hold her and say, "I love you Daisy. I know you want to play like you used to but be patient, until you're completely better."

22

As the days passed, Daisy started to heal. She has gotten really good at balancing on three legs and she doesn't fall to the side anymore. When Faith gets us out to play, Daisy runs faster and climbs higher than I do!

She still loves to eat raisins, chew on wood and do all the things she did before she lost her leg. Sometimes she even forgets she only has three legs...and so do I!

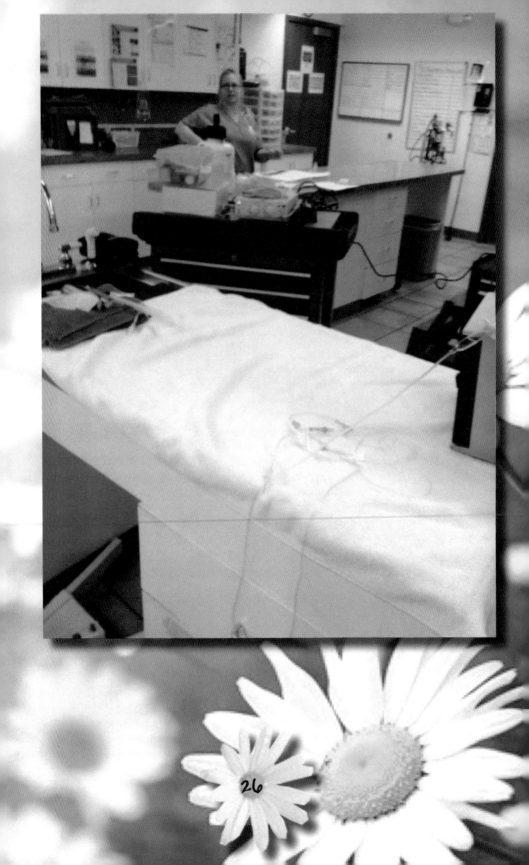

Daisy told me once how scared she was at the vet's office right before she had her surgery. They had to put her to sleep during the operation and she was afraid she might not wake up. But she trusted the doctors to take good care of her and they did.

I tell Daisy how brave she is and that sometimes I feel like it's my fault she got hurt, because I didn't protect her enough.

30

When I say that, she nibbles on my ear and whispers, "Sometimes accidents happen. The important thing is not to live in fear of accidents because if you do, you'll be afraid to live. And I'm still alive!"

We are in a new, safer chinchilla home now so Daisy and I will never have an accident like that again.

34

And Daisy still loves to laugh and jump and play. She's still Daisy, my best friend....and now my hero!

Best Friends

Hi, my name is Rosie, Daisy's
my best friend.
We will be together until the
very end.
We can't read or write and we
don't go to school,
'Cuz we are both chinchillas –
and that is pretty cool.

Our fur is soft and fluffy,
black but mostly gray.
We share a cage together, we
laugh and jump and play.
Yes, Daisy is my buddy, but
she's my hero too.
I don't think there's anything
that Daisy cannot do.

Now if you look at Daisy and then you look at me,
You'll see that I have four legs and Daisy has just three.
You might say she's handicapped, but then you would be wrong.
Don't feel sorry for her – 'cuz Daisy's awfully strong.

Anything I can do, Daisy can do too,
And when you read our story, you'll see just how that's true.
Never judge a person just by how they look.
That's the lesson to be learned – I hope you liked our book!

Daisy's Story

This is the true story of Daisy, our chinchilla. You may not know it, but chinchillas are very fragile. When they live in the wild, they live together in "packs." One chinchilla will keep watch while the others sleep. If a larger animal comes around that may try to hurt them, the chinchilla will "bark" to warn the others of danger. They cannot live in temperatures that are too warm, so if you have a chinchilla in your home the temperature has to be watched very carefully. If they get too hot, chinchillas can suffer from heat stroke.

When Daisy was less than a year old, she had a terrible accident. She

caught her foot in the cage and fell.
Her leg was broken too badly to fix.
Because chinchillas are so fragile, we
were very worried Daisy would not
live through the surgery to remove
her broken leg. But Daisy was strong
and spunky. Her doctor, Dr. Schmidt,
called her "Such a little trooper!"
We believe Daisy's spirit helped her
survive.

It's true that Daisy looks different on
the outside now. She looks different
than her best friend, Rosie, and other
chinchillas. And she looks different
than she used to – before the
accident. But different on the outside
doesn't mean she is different on the
inside. She is still strong...and spunky!
Daisy's story can help us understand

differences – not just between animals but also between people. We all have differences – some you can see easily and some you can't. Some of us are taller and some shorter. Some of us weigh more and some less. Some of us read faster or are good at math, while others are good at art or telling stories and jokes. Some of us have no arms or legs, while others have one or two. This story is about more than just accepting differences. It's about celebrating them. Our differences are what make us unique and interesting. What a boring world this would be if we were all exactly the same! There's only one Daisy. There's only one Rosie. And there's only one you!

Learn more about Daisy
and her life on her blog,
including additional pictures
and a free *Guide for Activities
and Discussion* for parents,
teachers, counselors and
mental health professionals at
www.therapiesinapod.com

About the Authors

Marney Studaker-Cordner and Kim Abraham are licensed Child and Family therapists in the Flint, Michigan area. They have provided therapeutic services and support to families dealing with concerns such as trauma, bullying, addiction, anxiety, depression, blended family and behavioral issues for over twenty five years. With backgrounds in child welfare, community mental health and early education, Marney and Kim have partnered to empower families, parents and children as they deal with the difficult issues facing society today. Marney and Kim have been contributing authors to the online parenting website

Empoweringparents.com since 2011. Their publications include the book, *The Whipped Parent: Hope for Parents Raising an Out-of-Control Teen* (Rainbow Books Inc, 2003) and the CD self-help programs *Life Over the Influence: What to do When Someone You Love Uses Drugs or Alcohol* and *The Oppositional Defiant Disorder (O.D.D.) Lifeline* (Legacy Publishing Company, 2011 and 2012).

Kim Abraham is a national speaker on the topics of Bullying, Childhood Behavior Disorders, Addiction and Parenting. She has been an expert guest on the HuffPost Live and NPR Morning Edition, as well as local radio and television news shows.

She holds certifications in Childhood Trauma Intervention, Trauma Debriefing, Grief and Loss Counseling and is an on-call volunteer for the American Red Cross.

Kim and Marney are available for one-on-one consultation, professional collaboration and speaking engagements. Please visit www.therapiesinapod.com for more information on our services and materials including parenting articles and resources. Parents, educators, counselors and mental health professionals will also find a free companion *Guide for Activities and Discussion* for Daisy's Story, to support children in learning about and embracing differences.

45

Made in the USA
San Bernardino, CA
18 March 2014